W9-CLX-991

SCIENCE ! SLEUTHS

?

QUESTION IT!

AZZA SHARKAWY

Crabtree Publishing Company

www.crabtreebooks.com

Author
Azza Sharkawy

Publishing plan research and development
Reagan Miller

Editors
Shirley Duke, Reagan Miller, Kathy Middleton

Proofreader
Shannon Welbourn

Indexer
Wendy Scavuzzo

Photo research
Katherine Berti

Design
Katherine Berti

Print and production coordinator
Katherine Berti

Photographs and illustrations
Thinkstock: Front Cover

All other images by Shutterstock

Library and Archives Canada Cataloguing in Publication

Sharkawy, Azza, author
      Question it! / Azza Sharkawy.

(Science sleuths)
Includes index.
Issued in print and electronic formats.
ISBN 978-0-7787-0759-2 (bound).--ISBN 978-0-7787-0784-4 (pbk.).--
ISBN 978-1-4271-7711-7 (pdf).--ISBN 978-1-4271-7705-6 (html)

      1. Curiosity--Juvenile literature. I. Title.

BF323.C8S43 2014   j153.8   C2014-903942-5
                                          C2014-903943-3

Library of Congress Cataloging-in-Publication Data

Sharkawy, Azza, author.
 Question it! / Azza Sharkawy.
    pages cm. -- (Science sleuths)
 Includes index.
  ISBN 978-0-7787-0759-2 (reinforced library binding) -- ISBN 978-0-7787-0784-4
(pbk.) -- ISBN 978-1-4271-7711-7 (electronic pdf) -- ISBN 978-1-4271-7705-6
(electronic html)
 1. Science--Methodology--Juvenile literature. 2. Research--Juvenile literature.
 I. Title.

 Q175.2.S53 2015
 507.2'1--dc23
                                          2014032325

Crabtree Publishing Company

www.crabtreebooks.com   1-800-387-7650

Printed in Canada/102014/EF20140925

Published in Canada
Crabtree Publishing
616 Welland Ave.
St. Catharines, Ontario
L2M 5V6

Published in the United States
Crabtree Publishing
PMB 59051
350 Fifth Avenue, 59th Floor
New York, New York 10118

Published in the United Kingdom
Crabtree Publishing
Maritime House
Basin Road North, Hove
BN41 1WR

Published in Australia
Crabtree Publishing
3 Charles Street
Coburg North
VIC 3058

CONTENTS

WHAT DO SCIENTISTS DO?

Have you ever looked up at the sky and wondered why it's blue? Or heard a splash in a pond and wondered what animal made the sound? Then you are thinking like a scientist! A scientist is someone who studies the **natural world**. The natural world is made up of all the **living** and **non-living** things around us. Scientists learn about the natural world by asking questions and exploring possible answers.

EXPLORE

We explore the world around us by using our **senses**. We have five senses. They are sight, smell, hearing, touch, and taste. Our senses help us **observe**, or get information about, things. The girl shown below is using her sense of touch to observe how a cat's fur feels. Is it soft and smooth or prickly and rough?

OBSERVE AND QUESTION

Scientists ask questions based on what they observe. The questions they ask help them to learn more about what they observe. For example, you might look at a snake and observe that it doesn't have legs. You might ask, "How does a snake move without any legs?" To help answer your question, you can observe the snake again and watch how it moves.

Observing may give you enough information to answer your question—or it may lead to more questions!

Questions help scientists learn about non-living things, too. What kinds of rocks feel smooth? How does the shape of the moon change each month? Are all metals shiny?

EXPLORE IT! ?

An observation is the information you get from using your senses. Read the two statements about zebras. Both statements are true, but only one is an observation. Which one do you think is *not* an observation? Explain your answer.

The zebra is black and white.

Zebras, horses, and donkeys belong to the same animal family.

SCIENTIFIC QUESTIONS

WHAT?

WHY?

HOW?

We ask many kinds of questions after we observe something. **Scientific questions** often begin with the words "what," "why," or "how." Questions that begin with these words make us think carefully about the things we observe. They lead us to the best way to answer the question. The answers to scientific questions describe or explain something about the natural world.

ANSWERS TO SCIENTIFIC QUESTIONS CAN BE FOUND IN MANY WAYS:

"How do crickets move around?"

You could find the answer by observing a cricket.

"Why do crickets chirp?"

You could find out in a book or ask an insect expert.

"Do crickets chirp less when it's cooler?"

Keep a cricket in a cage in a room and change the room's temperature. Count the number of chirps when it's warm and when it's cooler.

ASK THE RIGHT QUESTIONS

Not all questions are scientific questions. Scientific questions can be answered by doing a test. Non-scientific questions ask for simple information or how you feel about something. "What time does the soccer game start?" or "Do you like bananas?" are not scientific questions. You cannot do a test to find out when a game starts or why you like eating something.

HERE ARE SOME EXAMPLES OF SCIENTIFIC AND NON-SCIENTIFIC QUESTIONS:

Scientific questions:	Non-scientific questions:
Where do owls live?	Can I play outside?
What kinds of clouds bring rain?	Which park will we visit?
When are shadows the longest?	What animal makes the best pet?

EXPLORE IT!

?

Start a science journal. List things you can observe around you. Write questions you have about your observations. Add to the list as you think of new questions.

You can start your questions with:
I wonder why…? I wonder how…?
What would happen if...?
Does…?

I wonder how fish can breathe underwater?

What makes clouds?

What would happen if plants did not get sunlight?

TESTABLE QUESTIONS

Some questions about the natural world have already been answered. You can read books to find the answers to these questions. But there are still many questions that have not been answered. Scientists try to answer these questions by doing **investigations**.

An investigation is a way of gathering information by observing, planning, and doing a test.

This boy is doing an investigation to answer his scientific question: Will a bean plant grow taller in clay soil or in sandy soil?

A question is testable if it can be answered through the information gathered by observation. If a question cannot be answered by gathering information through observation, then it is not a testable question. Scientists write out testable questions to help them plan an investigation. To decide if a question is testable, it helps to ask: What can I do to find out…? A question is not testable if you have to ask for the answer or look it up in a book.

EXPLORE IT! **?**

Is "Do lizards live in Africa?" a testable question? (Hint: Can you easily travel to Africa and find out yourself?)

WHAT HAPPENS IF...?

Many scientific questions we ask begin with the word "Why?" But sometimes the answers to "why" questions can't be learned just by observing. "Why does a pumpkin float in water?" is not a testable question. Observing a pumpkin in the water won't tell you why it floats. You have to read or ask someone to learn why it floats. Changing the way you ask the question can help make it testable. Try to ask a question you can answer by observing. "What happens if you put a pumpkin in water?" You can test that question and find the answer—it floats!

DIFFERENT KINDS OF QUESTIONS

"What happens if…" is a good way to begin a question for investigation. Other good questions start with "How," " Does," and "I wonder." These kinds of questions help scientists get answers or learn more about something through observations. Different kinds of questions lead to different ways of learning things. They also lead to new questions!

EXPLORE IT!

Use the question starters on this page to change these statements into testable questions that can be observed.

A pumpkin with holes in it will sink in water.

Ice cubes melt faster in water than in the air.

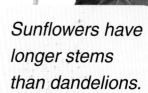

Sunflowers have longer stems than dandelions.

SO MANY QUESTIONS!

Scientists have learned so much about the natural world. But there is so much more we still need to learn. The more scientists learn about the world, the more questions they have. Every question that scientists answer can lead to more questions. Our work as scientists will never be finished. We will never run out of questions!

How many questions would you ask after watching a spider weave a web? You may ask, "Why does a spider weave a web?" and "Where does the **silk** for the web come from?" You can read a book to find the answers. These answers lead to new questions. "Do different spiders weave different web patterns?" "Are certain patterns stronger than others?" You can observe other webs to find these answers. Perhaps you can come up with a test to see how strong the different shapes are.

QUESTION WITH CARE

Scientists want to learn about the natural world. At the same time, they care about what they do to it. They make sure they ask questions that can be answered without harming the living things they want to observe. For example, if a scientist is studying how long it takes for a flower to bloom, a scientist would never pick the flower from the ground because this is harmful to the plant.

ASK THESE KINDS OF QUESTIONS BEFORE TESTING SOMETHING BY OBSERVING IT:

Is this a question
I can observe?

Is it safe to try to
answer this question?

Will answering this question
harm any living thing?

EXPLORE IT!

?

Is this a good question that can be tested? "Why do **mealworms** move quickly?" Why do you think it is or isn't?

IT TAKES PRACTICE

Asking testable questions takes practice. Share your questions with others. Talking about your questions often helps you figure out exactly what you are trying to find out. Others may have information that you don't, or be able to offer new ideas.

Scientists share their questions. Sharing lets them know if others have already tried to answer this question. It helps them ask the question in a clear way. Then they observe or test to learn the answer.

All scientists ask questions. They observe to find answers. They read and discuss their questions with other scientists. Observe your world. Ask some questions about it. You can be a scientist, too!

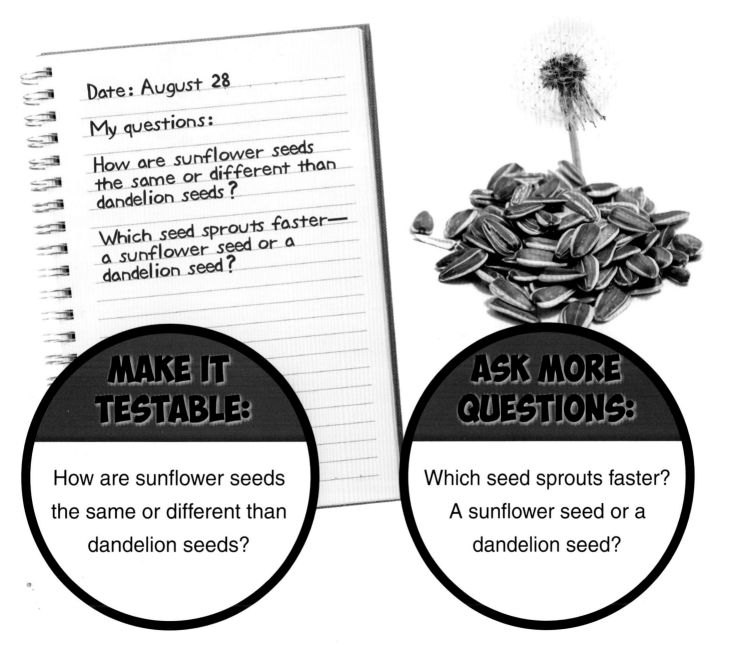

Date: August 28

My questions:

How are sunflower seeds the same or different than dandelion seeds?

Which seed sprouts faster—a sunflower seed or a dandelion seed?

MAKE IT TESTABLE:

How are sunflower seeds the same or different than dandelion seeds?

ASK MORE QUESTIONS:

Which seed sprouts faster? A sunflower seed or a dandelion seed?

OBSERVE, READ, QUESTION

Choose the question in each pair that is a good scientific question. Remember, they must be questions that are answered by an observation or test. Explain your answers.

Why does it thunder?

When does it thunder?

What do rain clouds look like?

What makes it hail during rainstorms?

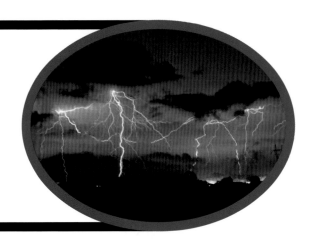

Change the last question to a good scientific question.

Non-scientific question: Do you like birds?

Non-scientific question: Why do birds fly?

Changed to scientific question:

LEARNING MORE

BOOKS

Investigating Your Backyard by Natalie Lunis. Newbridge Educational Publishing, 1999.

I Wonder Why Soap Makes Bubbles and Other Questions about Science by Barbara Taylor. Kingfisher, 2013.

Scientists Ask Questions: Physical Science by Ginger Garrett. Children's Press, 2005.

What is a Scientist? by Barbara Lehn. Lerner Publishing Group, 1998.

WEBSITES

This website presents a variety of interesting science questions and gives answers to them. **www.highlightskids.com/ science-questions**

This website helps you learn about different kinds of scientists and what they study. **http://pbskids.org/sid/ scientist.html**

In this website you will find a variety of science investigations, games, videos, and more. **www.sciencekids.co.nz/projects/ thescientificmethod.html**

GLOSSARY

investigations (in-ves-ti-GEY-shuhnz) noun Ways of gathering information by observing, planning, and doing tests

living (LIV-ing) adjective Alive; Plants and animals are examples of living things.

mealworms (MEEL-wurmz) noun Small, young forms of a beetle often eaten by birds

natural world (NACH-er-uhl WURLD) noun All living and non-living things in the world

non-living (non LIV-ing) adjective Not alive; Rocks and water are examples of non-living things.

observe (uhb-ZURV) verb To learn facts by using your senses

scientific questions (sahy-uhn-TIF-ik KWES-chuhnz) noun Questions that scientists ask to describe or explain the natural world

senses (SENS-ez) noun What we use to observe the natural world

silk (silk) noun The thin threads that come from a spider's body used to make a web

An adjective is a word that describes what something is like.
A noun is a person, place, or thing.
A verb is an action word that tells you what someone or something does.

INDEX